The Business Owner's Liquidity Solution

Taking Cash Out of Your Business While Keeping Control

Walter Lipski and David Ryan

The Business Owner's Liquidity Solution

Printed by:
90-Minute Books
302 Martinique Drive
Winter Haven, FL 33884
www.90minutebooks.com

Published in the United States of America

151231-00293

ISBN-13: 978-0692653098
ISBN-10: 0692653090

For more information on 90-Minute Books including finding out how you can publish your own lead generating book, visit www.90minutebooks.com or call (863) 318-0464

Here's What's Inside…

Introduction

When we first got started in Upton Financial Group, owners could sell their businesses and have confidence they could invest or use the proceeds from the sale of their business to generate income and financial security for their family. At that time, business owners were getting reasonable returns on their cash in the form of higher interest rates, and both the stock market and real estate were thought to be secure investments. Bottom line, after the business was sold, owners felt they always had a safe place to put their money.

Since the financial debacle that took place starting in late 2008 and continuing through 2009 and beyond, many business owners are still experiencing significant uncertainty about what to do for income in retirement, and also what to do with the money if they were to sell their company. Given the uncertainty of financial returns in today's environment for many business owners, the idea of giving up control is a paralyzing conundrum.

The previous thought process for many business owners was when it is time to retire, "I will sell my business, and the money I get from the sale will take care of my retirement." This thinking just doesn't work for most business owners in today's low interest, volatile stock market environment.

This is what drove us to create the Entrepreneurial Recap, or E-Recap. This is a liquidity solution that allows business owners to take cash out of their business today, maintain a majority equity position, and keep operating control over their business. Until recently, this type of financial structure was only available to companies valued at $50 million or more. Today, we will share with you how this same type of transaction structure can work for businesses valued at around $10 million or more.

In the current economy, which provides historic low-interest rates and an abundance of money that would like to be put to work, we at Upton have been able to show institutional capital investors a strategy for how they can put money to work in lower middle market-size businesses, i.e. companies with earnings starting around $1.5 million in EBITDA and greater. This opportunity has never been available before, and it's a real game-changer for business owners who want to keep active, would like significant liquidity today, and want to maintain control of their destiny.

The E-Recap provides business owners with liquidity today while they continue to control and operate their business. This liquidity provides financial security and helps alleviate some of the uncertainty in all business owners' thoughts having survived the recession of 2008 and 2009 and other world events.

Additionally, there is a shifting demographic; one business owner turns 65 every minute. Think about that. Many people are facing a transition; maybe not immediately, but definitely within the next three to five years. Rather than a business owner facing an all or nothing decision, e.g., either sell the business or keep it, the E-Recap allows business owners to phase in or complete their business ownership transition at their pace while taking significant wealth off the table and locking in financial security along the way.

In 2014, a CNBC survey showed that 70% of all small to mid-size business owners' wealth is tied up inside their business. It's no secret that privately held businesses for the most part are highly illiquid! Couple the high degree of illiquidity with the fact that many of today's business owners are approaching an age where they know they should plan for a transition in their companies, but are thinking, "I'm not ready to give up the income that I'm taking from my business because even if I sell it, I can't replace that income without side investments." They are stuck in what we call a 'liquidity trap', which really means illiquidity.

In meetings with business owners and their advisors (estate attorneys, business attorneys, accountants, and wealth advisors), the business owner often says:

- Gosh, I really need to fund a trust for my family's security.
- My wife and I would like to put more money towards our retirement.
- We would like to put money aside for our grandkids' education.
- We would like to pay off the house.

Etc., etc., etc. The list is limitless, but the answer usually includes, "But we can't do anything until we sell the business."

They are thinking of their situation as an either-or scenario when it comes to selling or keeping the business. We are here to show it doesn't have to be that way.

In fact, it can be just the opposite, with ample liquidity and operating control of the business. The opportunity for business owners and their wealth advisors to transform the biggest and most illiquid asset they have, their business, into a diversified financial portfolio is tremendous.

That's why we came up with the E-Recap. E-Recap helps you as a business owner to look at this from another point of view, and it provides a solution that you and your team may never have heard of before.

At the end of each chapter there is a chapter summary, and at the end of the book is a simple self-grading assessment to see if an E-Recap type structure is a good fit for you. Skip around the chapters or read from start to finish. We hope you enjoy our little book.

Our sincere objective in sharing this information is to help educate you and your advisors on a powerful solution that could help transition you from a position of huge illiquidity to one of financial diversification, all the while keeping control of your business.

To Your Success!

Walt Lipski & David Ryan

All of the illustrations and examples used in this book are for educational purposes only and neither represent nor guarantee any transaction outcomes or future results.

The Problems Caused by Lack of Liquidity for Business Owners

Business owners are often not ready to retire, but they want to truly reduce the exposure to the risk of running their business. They want to diversify their financial footprint and personal risk exposure.

When business owners nearing retirement age are asked why they don't jump on the retirement bandwagon right away or sell their business, the reason they most often give us is they don't want to give up control over their business.

While approaching age 65, a lot of business owners still have the 'fire in the belly'. They still want to work, they still want to create, but they realize the need to take some risks off the table. If they could get some liquidity, 'cash off the table', to finally unlock the toolbox of all their advisors, they could fund their way toward a better future; they could invest in the necessary estate planning they have been putting off, pay off the lake house, help their kid start a business, and build the financial security that lets them sleep well at night.

Some of the situations we run into:

A business owner that has three or four kids, but only one is working in the business. Question: how do you transfer the business to one kid and still keep the estate equitable for all? Maybe there is not enough life insurance or, due to age and/or health issues, purchasing more life insurance is not an option.

As the owner, what can you do? You can't give the business to one child and leave the other two or three siblings out in the cold, and you certainly don't want them having to approach the one sibling who is running the business to ask for money the rest of their lives. The liquidity solution we provide through an E-Recap is a much easier way to start funding your business transition strategy, retirement accounts, and long-term estate plans so they are all on a solid path forward and you will sleep well at night.

Another frequent scenario that gets played out is when management would like to buy the business. Many business owners truly want to transition the business to their top management person or team, almost as a reward. We frequently hear from owners that they were able to create the business and be successful because of their management team and the employees. So very often, business owners want to make sure the management team and/or key employees are taken care of as part of their transition out of the business.

There are several real challenges to selling the business to management. From the owner's perspective, they probably need and want a significant amount of the value of the business in cash to securely fund their retirement. This makes owner financing extremely limited or not an option at all. Basically the cash either has to come from the employee's personal savings or a bank loan. Most employees simply do not have the necessary large cash reserves required to purchase a business, and since most businesses are comprised of illiquid assets and considered 'collateral lite', raising enough money from a bank loan to finance selling to management is often doubtful.

Using an E-Recap strategy, we will show how we can accomplish the goal of selling to management while getting the necessary cash to securely fund retirement without requiring the business owner to personally guarantee the debt. Also, as an added side benefit, which we explain in a later chapter, there is an opportunity with the E-Recap to access additional working capital to help grow the business.

Please understand that when a business owner is required to personally guarantee the debt being taken out of the business, all they are doing is taking money from one pocket and putting it into the other pocket, because ultimately they are responsible for the repayment of debt. For business owners who are nearing retirement and working towards securing their financial future, personal guarantees should be avoided if at all possible.

How about using an E-Recap for an opportunistic acquisition? Consider this situation. One of our clients, George, age 59, has a profitable, growing $15 million annual revenue business. At the time we were talking to George and his advisors about generating some liquidity for long-term estate planning options, a similar size competitor with very little overlap in customers and products approached him at an industry trade show and said, "George, I'm 72 years old. I really would like to sell and phase out of my business over the next 18 months."

This was a perfect opportunity for George to get recommitted to his business for several more years, virtually double the revenue, and more than double the earnings due to synergies between the companies. We looked at George's company from the perspective of an E-Recap, creating liquidity to acquire his competitor while at the same time creating a significant nest egg of liquidity for George to secure and diversify his personal financial footprint. This monetizing of George's business, combined with having an institutional partner, gave George the confidence to put a strategy in place to buy his competitor in a truly win-win deal.

Chapter Summary:

An E-Recap strategy is very flexible. At Upton, we work with entrepreneurs to create a liquidity event within their businesses tailored to funding their specific goals and objectives. An added benefit of an E-Recap is it allows entrepreneurs to diversify their wealth out of the business while at the same time keeping them in control and retaining majority ownership. This is key.

The E-Recap Is a Flexible Liquidity Solution

At Upton Financial Group, we use many of the same tools used by private equity to acquire businesses. When a traditional private equity deal is in process, it becomes apparent that the private equity firm will end up with the majority (70-80%) of equity and control, while claiming that the business owner retains a 'significant interest', approximately 20-30%. With the E-Recap, we follow a similar process but reverse the roles, so the business owner retains more control over the amount of debt that is put on the business as well as keeping 60-75% of the ownership and the financial upside.

This is a very important distinction with the E-Recap. As time progresses, the business owner, not the private equity group, continues to run and operate the business because he has control and also has majority ownership, which means he also receives the lion's share of the upside going forward. Since the upside compounds, with the E-Recap structure, the owner is able to have 60-75% compounding control versus 20-30% compounding with the traditional private equity deal. Another benefit with the E-Recap, the owner will have reduced their personal exposure to the risks of running the business by taking significant money off the table and also freeing themselves from personal guarantees often associated with business ownership.

The E-Recap should be reviewed as an alternative (or at least used as a comparison tool) when one is considering a sale to a private equity group or an ESOP. The E-Recap is truly a powerful and remarkable tool for providing the business owner liquidity while maintaining majority ownership and control.

Years ago, one of our clients asked us, "Why should I sell my business if I'm going to do an ESOP and get all the proceeds tax-free?" Walt said to him, "Look, Eric, please call the ESOP company and ask them if your name is required to be on a personal guarantee, as an ESOP will often require bank debt." The prospective client replied, "They told me no, that it's my money." Walt said, "Go and ask them specifically if you will be named on a personal guarantee." The gentleman called back within three hours and said, "I want to sell the company because you were right." This business owner became a client and we sold their business to an industry buyer. At the time, the E-Recap structure was not available to smaller, mid-market size companies.

The idea of personal guarantees at the time of retirement, once you have left the day-to-day operations and control of the business in the hands of others, is a very difficult and potentially risky arrangement. As one business owner told us, "I don't ever want to come back as a Walmart greeter." Business owners really need the security of moving from lack of liquidity to financial certainty.

Chapter Summary

The E-Recap is a unique solution that fits itself to each company's unique circumstances. Circumstances differ because everyone generally wants to accomplish something a little different. The take-away is that the E-Recap is an extremely flexible liquidity solution.

When a business owner employs the E-Recap process, they can:

- Harvest 60-75% of the value of their company in cash today.
- Use the cash for most any objective they have.
- Maintain majority control.
- Receive the majority of the upside from the business going forward.
- As a bonus, gain the liquidity without having to sign personal guarantees at the bank, i.e., the ESOP.

The E-Recap Works for Many Different Businesses by Using a Blend of Debt and Minority Equity

While we are talking in generalities, we know that it is important to view each business as its own unique entity, just as each person is unique.

In our initial meeting with business owners, one of the first questions we like to ask up front is, "Imagine we are starting with a clean piece of paper. Now, please describe or sketch for us in your own words the most ideal transition, both personally and professionally, from your business, whether it's in the next six months, a year, or five to seven years from now."

We need to start with the business owner and his spouse and understand what they want to accomplish and then see how these tools will work.

Let's start with the basics. If you want to harvest some money from your business, it can only come in one of two forms: debt or equity. There is no other alternative.

The idea behind the E-Recap is that we use a blend of both debt and equity so we can accomplish significant liquidity, i.e., 60-75% of the value of the business. It is important that in order for the business owner to retain control, they must hold on to the majority of the equity, at least 51%, meaning an owner can sell from 1% to 49% of the equity and still maintain majority control.

Next, the idea is to bring in a major portion of the liquidity proceeds in debt. Not just any debt; the goal is to use *institutional* non-recourse debt if at all possible. Non-recourse debt means that once the money is distributed to the business owner that money is 'off the table', meaning creditors of the business cannot access the proceeds. This is important because in the normal course of running a business, things happen—people get hurt, products just don't function right, etc., etc.

One of the keys behind the E-Recap is finding a single source capital provider, meaning the capital source funding the E-Recap provides both the non-recourse debt and buys the minority equity stake in the company. While this is not always attainable, it is one of the points on which we focus because it helps to align everyone's interests.

The E-Recap, properly deployed, can be a tax-efficient tool for the business owner to receive the proceeds from the transaction. While everyone's tax situation will be different, an important objective is maximizing the after-tax cash the owner (i.e., the entrepreneur) receives. At the end of the day, it does not matter how large the offer or how high the price, what matters most is how much money a business owner nets in his pocket after taxes.

We could talk all day about different recaps and scenarios, but at this point, a simplified example modeled after a company we worked with may be most helpful for readers to clearly see and identify themselves in the different roles.

The company in our example is a niche manufacturing company with two 50% owners who both work in the business.

Sam is 63 years old, and he and his wife are 'empty nesters'—their kids are grown and have successful careers of their own. The grandkids live out of state, and Sam and his wife enjoy seeing them as often as they can. Ideally, Sam would like to slow down. He really wants to take his equity out of the business and retire. The last thing he wants to do is keep feeding the business the additional working capital required to support and grow the business.

Bill, on the other hand, is 52 years old. He needs a number of good earning years in his future because he is still raising kids at home. He has college tuition and weddings in the future along with other goals that require large expenditures.

So in addition to having time on his side, Bill has the desire, the fire in his belly, to really grow the business. The fact that Sam is reluctant to commit more capital to the long-term growth opportunities for the business is becoming a potential concern for Bill.

Ideally, Bill would like to increase his ownership equity, see Sam successfully transition out of the business, take some money out of the business to begin locking in some financial security for his family, and be free to aggressively implement his plans for growing the business.

How might an E-Recap work for Sam and Bill?

Let's look at the numbers. See Figure 1 on the next page, understanding that for this example the financial parameters have been simplified.

Sam and Bill's company has earnings of $2 million in EBITDA. EBITDA is a term that means Earnings before Interest, Taxes, Depreciation, and Amortization, and is used as a proxy term for 'cash flow'.

(Note some industries and companies have high capital expenditure requirements and/or high seasonal debt and other factors that may need to be taken into consideration. For the purposes of this illustration, we are not addressing these factors.)

Figure 1:

Assumptions used in the Example ($mm):

Company Valuation	
EBITDA	$ 2.00
Multiple	5.00 x
Enterprise Value	**$ 10.00**
Sources of Capital	
Debt	$ 6.00
Rollover Equity - Bill	3.00
New Equity -Institutional	1.00
Total	**$ 10.00**
Uses of Capital	
Cash Distribution	$ 7.00
Rollover Equity	3.00
Total	**$ 10.00**

To summarize, we have a $2 million dollar EBITDA company. For this example, we will use a valuation multiple of EBITDA of five (5.0 x). This gives us a business enterprise value of $10 million ($2 million EBITDA times 5 multiple).

According to a recent Market Pulse report, a 5 times multiple of EBITDA was mid-range for a solid performing lower middle market manufacturing company. Multiples vary greatly based on industry, quality of the company, growth potential, and many factors too numerous for this discussion.

Now, let's walk through what happens to our two 50% owners. Ideally, Sam wants to take his ‘cash and dash’; he really needs the cash to secure his retirement. First, we need a plan that will give Sam $5 million (tax advantaged) for his 50% of the business.

The typical solutions to this challenging scenario for Bill prior to the E-Recap being available were:

1. To do nothing and just live with the situation until it eventually blows up,
2. Join Sam in selling the whole company and find something else to do,
3. Try and strike an 80/20 deal in a typical private equity transaction,
4. Or try and raise the $5 million needed to buy out Sam by borrowing as much as he can at the bank, dipping into personal savings, loading up on personal guarantees, and hoping Sam will take a note for part of the consideration.

None of the above approaches really accomplish Sam and Bill's original goals. In Sam's case, he may or may not get all the cash he needs up front to secure his retirement. However, in Bill's case, each of the above approaches to varying degrees put all the risk on Bill without the prospects of much upside for many years.

Consider, for example, the scenario where Bill wants to try and raise the money to buy Sam out. Rather than putting money in his pocket, he is most likely taking some out. Clearly any hopes of putting money aside to begin securing his and his family's financial security just took a back seat to buying out Sam. Further, he will be up to his eyeballs in both bank and personal debt, all tied to personal guarantees. The only thing Bill will have is 100% of the equity, as long as he pays his notes, operational control to the extent he does not breach any bank covenants, limitations on the amount of money he can borrow to fund the company's growth, and finally, he has all the risk. This is a typical scenario of what an old school traditional partner buy out looks like.

With the E-Recap, by contrast, we can raise enough money so that Sam is paid off and gone, and Bill, who wants to remain and still has the fire in the belly, can take $2 million in cash, tax advantaged, off the table so he and his wife can start building their retirement nest egg, and he will own 75% of the company without the huge burden of personal guarantees on the debt while having an institutional capital partner who can provide additional growth capital.

How are we going to do that? As you will see in the illustration, we are using a combination of non-recourse debt and the sale of 25% equity.

Under the section Sources of Capital in Figure 1, we are proposing to use non-recourse debt that is approximately a 3 multiple of EBITDA, which will produce $6 million worth of cash (3 times $2 million EBITDA). This debt often has a unique characteristic that makes it different than commercial bank debt because it is not amortized. However, if the business does have the available extra cash, there is no prepayment penalty. In essence, we're renting that debt, if you will, which allows management to make the best determination of where and how to deploy the working capital and the resources of the business. So this is very, very powerful capital.

With $6 million worth of debt on the business that was worth $10 million, that leaves the business with something called a 'net equity value' of $4 million, ($10 million valuation [enterprise value] less the $6 million of non-recourse debt). The next step is to sell 25% of that $4 million in remaining equity, raising an additional $1 million. This shows up under the Sources of Capital as $1 million in the table as 'New Equity Institutional'. See Figure 1.

Moving down to the next section in the table under Uses of Funds, we can see where there is $7 million available for Cash Distribution. The first $5 million goes to Sam to buy out his equity in the company, then $2 million goes to Bill, and Bill will then roll over his $3 million in remaining equity.

To summarize, post-close the company has a $4 million 'net equity value'. Bill is holding $3 million or

75% ownership, and he has an institutional financial partner that owns $1 million or 25% ownership of the company. This allows the business to stay financially healthy while allowing both business owners to accomplish their objectives.

At this point, if I were a business owner, I would be thinking, "Okay, so we worked through this, but what did I accomplish by using the E-Recap?" See Figure 2 below.

Figure 2:

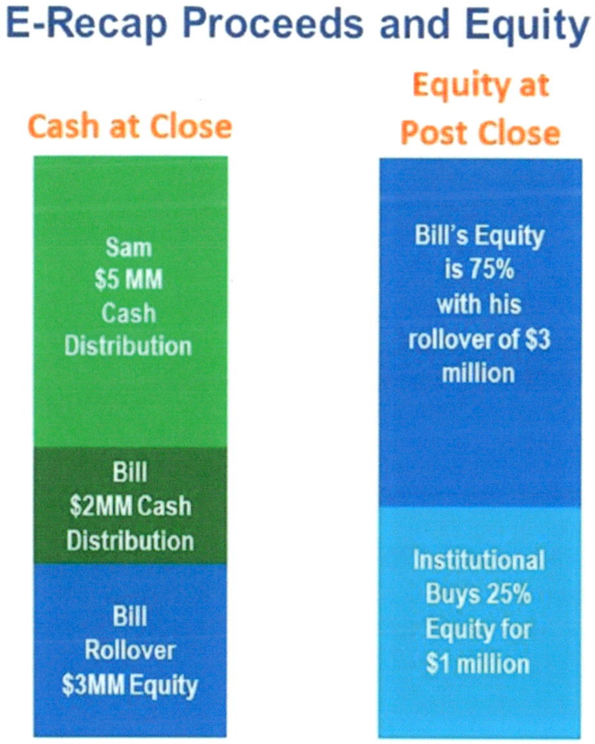

Sam was able to take his $5 million and leaves happy, without any notes or strings attached. That is a huge advantage to the remaining business owner, in this case Bill.

When a company is saddled with a partner who doesn't want to grow the business anymore, and just wants to keep things status quo and collect a check, especially when the company is opportunistically poised to grow, the situation potentially works like cancer on the business over time. The sooner the reluctant partner can be dealt with the better, because opportunity is perishable. If not acted on in a timely fashion, usually a competitor or some other group will act on it and the significant hopeful upside impact is lost forever.

For Bill, see Figure 2. We took $2 million off the table that Bill and his financial advisor can put to work in various investments outside the business. Bill's spouse is sitting at home and thinking, "Wow, we are actually funding the various vehicles that will secure our long-term retirement." As far as personal risk, well, guess what? Bill was able to take off a chunk of money, while also letting go of his reluctant partner. He has replaced his previous 50% ownership for 75% ownership, with institutional capital behind the company, and he did all this without signing personal guarantees.

Now, when the company makes money over and above debt service, Bill and his institutional partner share distributions 75%-25%. Rather than getting distributions of 50% of the profits, Bill is now getting 75% of the profits, and he has full operating control.

Chapter Summary

This chapter lays out by example each step of how the E-Recap transaction structure works. Even the Cliff Notes version would probably encourage you to read the whole chapter.

The liquidity generated by the E-Recap process comes from a blend of non-recourse debt and the sale of minority equity.

Minority equity is defined as 1-49% ownership; typically, an E-Recap minority equity is between 25 and 40%.

Non-recourse debt attributes:

- Non-amortizing interest only
- No prepayment penalty
- No personal guarantees required

The ideal situation is for the debt and equity source to be the same capital provider because it truly aligns ownership and financial partner interest. This is not always possible, but something we work diligently to make happen.

The E-Recap leaves the business owner with operating control and the lion's share of the distribution of profits after debt service going forward.

E-Recap vs. a Traditional Private Equity Transaction

Let's compare a traditional private equity transaction to an E-Recap transaction structure to summarize the benefits shown in the previous example. Let's use the same business that was valued at $10 million in the example and has earnings of $2 million of EBITDA.

Figure 3 below contrasts the two approaches.

Figure 3

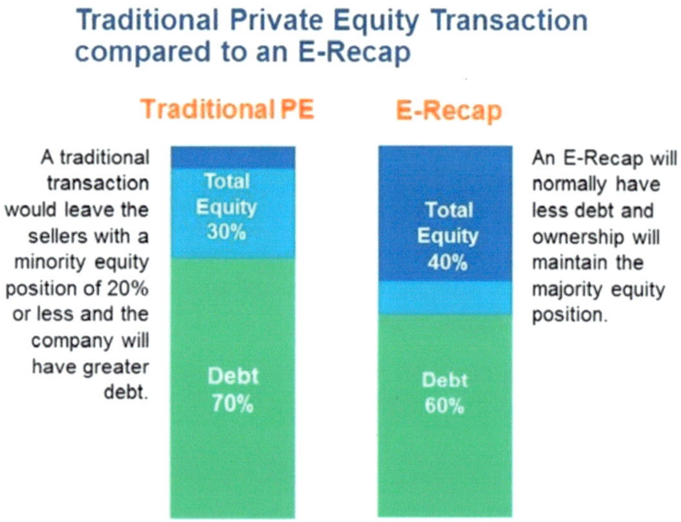

Typically, a traditional private equity firm will want controlling interest (most do), and will propose a structure putting debt of around 3.5 times the $2 million of EBITDA on the business. The private equity firm will generally borrow 70% of that $10

million ($7 million total, using both senior and sub debt), then they will hold 80% of the equity and have the remaining ownership roll over equity equal to 20% of the remaining net equity value of $3 million ($600,000 total). However, as the selling owner, you will only retain 20% of your company going forward.

In the example you can see in the E-Recap illustration on the previous page, Figure 3, we only put on 60% of debt in the E-Recap process. We picked up another $1 million by selling 25% of the remaining net equity to the institutional investor. In the illustration, you can begin to see the impact of having 75% ownership. You are in control, and you're getting 75% of the distributions going forward.

This is why we call it the Entrepreneurial Recap. The *entrepreneur* is in control and maintains all of the benefits of ownership while receiving the benefit of liquidity.

Some business owners may be a bit more averse to debt than others. Staying with our example, instead of using 60% debt and selling a 25% minority equity stake, a deal could possibly be struck using only 50% debt and selling a 40% minority equity stake, which would accomplish virtually the same liquidity outcome. The point to remember is the E-Recap is a blended transaction using debt and minority equity. Maybe you don't need to take out $7 million to accomplish the ownership objectives, possibly you just need $6 million; these details can all be tailored to a specific business. We like to think of this particular stage as the 'first bite of the apple'.

To provide an overview on private equity, just who are these institutional capital firms?

In North America, there are approximately 2,900 private equity groups of all sizes according to Private Equity Info. About half, around 1,400, are ‘funded’ private equity groups. This means these groups have ready access to funds; they can make an investment decision, write the check, and go. Unfunded groups find a deal and then try to raise the financing. We focus on working with funded groups.

A couple of years ago, when we realized the possibilities of the E-Recap and put this model together, we extensively researched and reviewed the 1,400 or so firms making up the funded private equity universe.

Our parameters were:

- Needed to be a funded group
- Will do minority transactions
- Have the ability to do sole-source funding (i.e. provide both the debt and equity portion of the deal, which offers this tremendous flexibility plus a true partner on the board).

We have identified around 30 private equity groups out of that list of around 1,400 groups who will entertain an E-Recap type of transaction for lower middle market size companies.

Recognizing that the E-Recap is not a one-size-fits-all solution, should you as the business owner decide it could be a good fit for you, we will work with you to position your business in its best light and then seek out a number of suitable institutional groups to approach. Our goal in bringing an E-Recap opportunity to market is to create a competitive process around which institutional capital competes for your company. In this way, we create leverage to negotiate the best transaction structure to meet your ultimate goals and objectives and needs.

Chapter Summary

Both the traditional private equity deal and an E-Recap transaction incorporate a level of debt in their respective deal structures.

The E-Recap typically uses significantly less debt than a traditional private equity deal.

The E-Recap is a flexible structure; traditional private equity is less flexible and more narrowly structured.

Out of about 2,900 total private equity firms in North America, there are approximately 1,400 that are 'funded' groups, and of those there are about 30 who are capable of 'one source funding' and will do lower middle market size minority transactions.

One source funding means the capital source will provide both the non-recourse debt and purchase the minority equity.

The Second Bite of the Apple

Staying with our Sam and Bill example, let's assume it is now five years later. Bill is running the company and both the company and Bill's relationship with his institutional partner are going well. Bill and his financial planner meet and they determine if Bill sold his interest in the company today, those proceeds, along with his other assets outside the company, would allow Bill and his wife to retire comfortably.

The illustration on the following page, Figure 4, captures the importance and power of the 'second bite of the apple' strategy.

Figure 4

The Second Bite of the Apple

Future Impact to Bill and his Institutional Investor

Assumptions Going Forward	
Timeline:	5 Years
Annual Revenue Growth:	12.0%
Avg EBITDA Margins:	12.2%

2nd Liquidity Event ($mm)	
Projected EBITDA:	$ 3.70
Multiple at exit:	5.75 x
Enterprise Value	**$21.26**

Looking at the table above, after five years, assuming the business continued its average historical revenue growth of 12% and average earning margins of 12.2%, the projected EBITDA is expected to be $3.7 million. The company went from $2 million to $3.7 million EBITDA under Bill's guidance over the past 5 years.

This increase in EBITDA will certainly translate into increase in the value of the company. Additionally, as a company grows and gets larger, the valuation multiple of EBITDA increases. In this example, we are using a conservative multiple increase of .75 (so we increased the valuation multiple from 5 to 5.75). There are two reasons for the multiple increase. One, the company has continued to grow and now has a higher level of earnings and is more desirable to buyers. Two, the company will have been working with a professional board for the last five years. We call this taking your business to 'finishing school'. More on this later in this chapter.

Figure 5 on the following page, compares what would happen had the owners sold initially for $10 million rather than using the E-Recap. If the company had just been sold outright five years ago, Sam and Bill would have each received $5 million. By using the E-Recap, however, Sam got his $5 million and left (so no difference), while Bill rolled over his $3 million in equity. The funding source put in their $1 million dollars of equity. Five years later, the business has profitably grown and the enterprise value is now $21.26 million ($3.7 million EBITDA times a 5.75 multiple). Remember, the $6 million of debt from the original E-Recap has been paid off through the normal course of operations, so now the proceeds, $21.26 million, are split 75% to Bill and 25% to the institutional investor.

Figure 5:

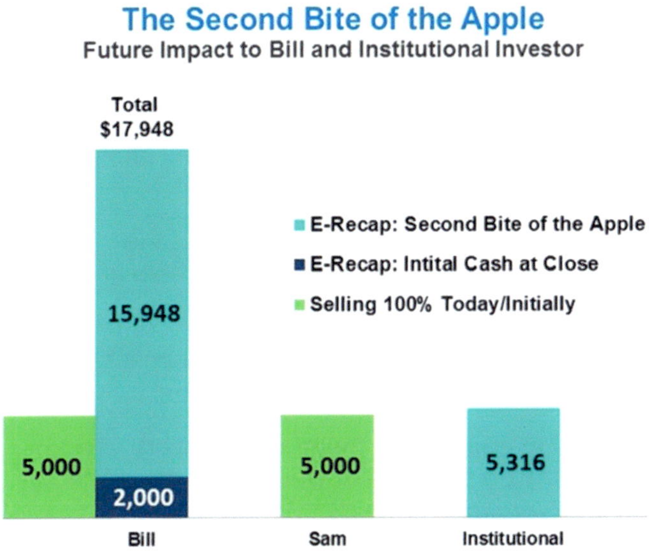

Rather than taking $5 million for his share of the company five years ago, Bill took $2 million in cash and rolled his remaining equity for a 75% ownership stake in the company. On the second sale, or 'second bite of the apple', he then got an additional $15.9 million for a total return of almost $18 million. The institutional financial partner got the original debt they lent paid back through the operation of the company, and their initial equity of $1 million grew to $5.3 million, shoulder to shoulder, with Bill. See Figure 5.

How did the E-Recap impact Bill?

- In the initial E-Recap, he was able to take $2 million off the table.
- He got free of Sam, his old partner, on equitable terms and without any strings attached.
- He was able to retain control of the company and grow it with the help of his institutional partner.
- Personally, he did not saddle himself or his estate with personal guarantees.
- He was able to maintain his salary while he took advantage of working for the additional 5 years.
- He was able to receive 75% of the distributions of profits vs. only 50% before.
- But the 'second bite of the apple' was HUGE for Bill. He got an additional $15.9 million, almost 8 times his original liquidity check.
- And he accomplished all of the above with less risk.

The 'second bite of the apple' is truly breaking the company through the glass ceiling, taking advantage of the longer runway (timeframes) that Bill had and Sam didn't have. In most cases, it is much more beneficial for the shareholder who is not ready to leave to utilize an E-Recap and maintain control.

The illustrations used in this example make clear the alignment of interests of the business owner and the institutional capital partner throughout the life of the arrangement.

Let us share some thoughts on taking your business to 'finishing school'.

The majority of businesses valued at over $5 million are either sold to private equity groups or sold to companies that are backed by private equity groups (around 60% according to the June 2015 Market Pulse Report).

When a business that is linked with an institutional partner goes to market, it becomes more desirable for a couple of reasons. First, there is the perception of less risk since the buyer will know the financial reporting will be at a higher standard and is likely more transparent. Secondly, the management team is seen as a group that can work well with an institutional partner.

We didn't immediately realize this, but over time we have seen where businesses that have an institutional partnership generally trade at higher multiples. When you have a true institutional investor at your side, you as the business owner are really taking your business to 'finishing school' and building your ultimate exit.

Chapter Summary

Please review the chart and the bullet points under "How did the E-Recap impact Bill?" section above, Figures 5 and 6.

The Mistakes Business Owners Often Make

We see business owners make a number of mistakes, and we will share a few in the hopes of preventing others from repeating them.

First, business owners make the initial start more of a problem than it really is; the problem becomes larger than life.

Generally, business owners are trying to achieve 'financial freedom', meaning they want to ensure they have enough income from their investable assets to take care of their current lifestyle and their projected long-term needs. As we have seen, for most business owners, their business represents nearly 70% of their total net worth. That begs the question, "How much is enough?"

This is where the E-Recap can be a good jump-start if implemented five to seven years before your anticipated retirement. As we have shown, you will have the cash working outside the business growing and funding your retirement; meanwhile, the company continues under your management, as you are the majority owner taking your salary plus the majority of any distributions.

The solution is for business owners to slow down and understand what they truly need in terms of financial assets.

We have seen a number of instances where the business owners think what they need so much greater than the amount they truly need. That's why we frequently work with financial planners and wealth advisors. As a business owner, if you don't have a financial plan, we really encourage you to get one. At the end of the day, a business owner needs to understand how much money it will take and where it will come from for them to fund the next chapter of their life.

Any transaction, an outright sale or an E-Recap strategy, should be part of the overall financial plan. If a transaction or liquidity event does not help accomplish the owner's goals, the question becomes, "Why do it?"

We look at this process as being a two-step approach. The first step is to simply review and analyze where the business is today. Define your starting point.

Once that is done, your wealth advisor and other professionals can assist you in taking a holistic approach to your financial future, incorporating savings, investments, and the current realistic value of your business. Only after knowing the value and possible liquidity options for your business today and incorporating the assets outside your business in your overall financial plan can your advisors and confidants (i.e. professional advisors, spouse, family members) provide you the data points you need to make smart decisions regarding your financial future.

We had one financial advisor review a plan we put together utilizing an E-Recap structure to create significant liquidity. When we all got together, the advisor looked at their client and said, "Look, if you come in anywhere close to this liquidity target amount, based on your other assets, you don't need to work a day of your life again." Bottom line, if you have enough liquidity outside the business, then you can work for the fun of it.

It's important to start the dialogue early on. As we pointed out earlier, something that is revealed time after time by participants in our seminars is that a lot of owners are holding on to the business because they don't want to give up control. They often think in terms of an all-or-nothing case; "I either sell 100% of the business, or I don't sell it and I keep it all." The E-Recap offers business owners the opportunity to change that ‘all or nothing’ mindset and explore creating liquidity today while keeping control.

Another common mistake is an owner’s belief that they must sell 100% of their company or take no action at all.

To illustrate this point, three brothers were partners in a manufacturing business in a small town that employed between 90 and 100 people. The company had been in operation for over 27 years and had a very good product. They were contacted by several industry players, a few who had private equity backing, and all who wanted to acquire their business.

We were introduced to the owners after the traditional private equity group deal had failed. Why? Because the owners realized that if they sold out either to a competitor or to a private equity group, they would only retain a small minority ownership of around 20% and thus would no longer have operational control of the business.

While the brothers liked the idea of their older brother cashing out and retiring comfortably, and they liked the fact they could each take some chips off the table, they could not get comfortable losing operating control.

At the core of their concern was the fear that a new buyer would want to roll them up or combine their operations in to a larger organization. They feared this would result in the loss of jobs for their nearly 100 employees. These employees were the sons and daughters of people with whom these owners went to high school. They just couldn't enter into a deal that had the potential to devastate their local community. This is just one example of how the issue of control can manifest itself. Fortunately, we have a way around that using the E-Recap strategy.

Chapter Summary

As a business owner, if you do not have an experienced wealth advisor, consider getting one.

Put together a financial plan that incorporates both a realistic valuation of your business in today's market and explore how much liquidity could be locked up in your business today.

Taking the above two steps will go a long way toward giving you confidence when making any future business transition decisions.

Big Myths that Business Owners Often Believe

Many business owners believe that by selling a portion of their company they will lose operational control, which, as we have shown, is not the case.

This is an understandable misconception since the majority of deals are done as 'traditional' *complete* acquisitions by a competitor (who may or may not be part of a private equity company). Most owners believe they will lose control because they are getting money for something.

We really fight that myth because many advisors come back to us (even before the process is allowed to get going) and say, "No, the owner is going to have debt. There will be covenants that restrain the owner's ability to run the business, and these covenants mean they will lose control of their company."

Remember, we get the institution lined up as capital partners right alongside our business owners, so yes, there will be covenants signed because institutions don't want owners to add outside debt that will be given a position in front of them, but the issue of 'loss of operational control' is still a myth.

There is another myth that we always run into – the cost is too high. Really!

Owners need to remember that when they sell the business, that's the ultimate cost of capital because they are no longer getting a return for what they sold. It's gone. Sometimes, owners turn around and say, "Okay, we'll keep it." Well, there is a cost involved in keeping that ownership because most business owners personally guarantee all the credit of the business, so owners are also exposed to any or all of the liabilities that come with the business regardless of the security of that corporate shell.

That risk needs to be measured in a manner we call 'doubling down', in which the owner's personal assets as well as the business assets are guaranteeing the business. In other words, all of the business owner's assets, both personal and the business, are generally exposed to the risks of operating their business. While you can't quite put an exact dollar amount on risk, again, we believe this idea of too-high cost is a myth. Just because you can't measure it doesn't mean it's not a real risk.

The other issue about the business is just the fact that its value is illiquid. So as the business grows, your illiquidity grows, and illiquidity is a huge factor with all of the various risks that are possible in the current business environment.

Chapter Summary

Misconceptions about business valuation and deal structures abound. What may have worked for your friend Charlie when he sold his company may not be at all applicable to your situation.

Every business sale or liquidity transaction is unique to the business owner and the goals and objectives they wish to accomplish.

Starting with the financial realities of your business, i.e., a realistic valuation and amount of potential liquidity in your business, coupled with a good experienced team of professional advisors (wealth advisor, business intermediary, CPA and attorney), will help you confidently and successfully exit from your business on your terms.

How to Take Cash Out of Your Business While Maintaining Control

We understand that an E-Recap isn't suitable for every company. To help determine if an E-Recap is a good fit for YOU and your business, we have included on the following pages a simple self-grading assessment that you can fill out in the comfort of your own home, in the privacy of your own thoughts.

After adding up your scores from all six questions, compare your score to the scenarios in the "How did you do?" section. We truly believe that after reading this book and taking the survey, you'll understand the subject better. You will know whether an E-Recap could be a good fit for you.

If it's a good fit for you now, we encourage you to give us a call so that we can talk (confidentially) about your situation. We will work with you to figure out the next steps to gather data and move forward. The process starts with taking the survey; think about it and give us call. We would love the opportunity to be of value.

We do not look for engagements, and we do not look for listings. We look for opportunities to help people achieve their dreams. If that just happens to involve the transition of a business, then we get really excited because that is what we do best.

You can reach us at: Upton Financial Group, phone 480-499-5556 in Scottsdale or 707-546-7860 in Santa Rosa.

E-Recap Assessment

How ready is your business for an E-Recap?

Answer the questions to the best of your ability:

1. How long do you expect to continue to have ownership and control of your business?
    - More than 7 years: 10 points
    - 3 to 7 years: 5 points
    - Less than 3 years: 0 points

Score: ___________

2. What is your total annual revenue?
    - More than $20 million: 10 points
    - $5 million to $20 million: 5 points
    - Less than $5 million: 0 points

Score: _________

3. What is your adjusted EBITDA for the most recent year?
    - More than $2 million: 10 points
    - $1.5 to $2 million: 5 points
    - Less than $1.5 million: 0 points

Score: __________

4. What is your company's long-term debt?
    - Less than 1.5 times your adjusted EBITDA: 10 points
    - 1.5 to 2.5 times your adjusted EBITDA: 5 points
    - Great than 2.5 times your adjusted EBITDA: 0 points

Score: __________

5. Is your company and/or its shareholders required to provide completion bonds or similar guarantees in order to perform work?
    - Yes: 0 points
    - No: 10 points

Score: __________

6. Does any one single customer represent more than 10% of annual gross revenue of the company?

    - Yes — 0 points
    - No — 10 points

Score: __________

How did you do?

60 – 45: Your Company is likely a perfect candidate for an E-Recap, and you should move quickly to complete a feasibility report.

45 – 30: Your Company is probably a good prospect for an E-Recap; you should explore further with a phone call to better understand your unique situation and whether there is a fit.

Below 30: Your Company is probably not a good candidate for an E-Recap at this time. However, if you expect your score to improve within the next 12 months, you might still consider having an exploratory conversation.

About the Authors

Walter L. Lipski

Walt brings his entrepreneurial experience and perspective to his client's investment banking transactions. In 1980, Walt founded an energy control manufacturing firm serving the global hospitality industry. In 1992, Walt sold his company to a public company where he was responsible for integrating and managing world-wide sales and marketing teams across multiple acquisitions.

Over the last 22 years, Walt has used his entrepreneurial experience and energies to help owners of privately held middle market companies, across many industries, realize their transition and liquidity goals through business sales, acquisitions and recapitalizations.

Walt is a nationally recognized speaker at professional meetings and conventions on topics ranging from business sales, acquisitions and M&A negotiation strategies. Walt is the 2006 recipient of the Darrell Fouts award, the most prestigious award given by the M&A Source (the largest association of M&A intermediaries) in recognition of his contributions to the profession.

Walt has held board level positions in state, national and international professional organizations, including past chair of the M&A Source. In 2008, he served as co-chair of this organization's Strategic Initiative Task Force on Security Licensing, and was instrumental in the SEC's issuing of a landmark "CBI No Action Letter." Walt currently serves on the online education committee for the M&A Source.

David G. Ryan

David Ryan has more than 25 years of experience in the Mergers & Acquisitions industry. He has initiated and completed a wide range of mergers, acquisitions, sales and financings for an extensive range of clients.

David's previous experience as a practicing CPA (Certified Public Accountant), CVA (Certified Valuation Analyst) and investor has proven to be an ideal background to work with buyers, sellers and their representatives in structuring and completing transactions. David was the 2015 recipient of the Darrell Fouts Award, an award granted by the M&A Source for his visionary leadership and exceptional contributions to the professional association.

David's activity in professional organizations include past chair of the M&A Source (the largest association of middle market intermediaries), past co-chair of the Midmarket Expo (where he worked with over 150 private equity groups), and member of the American Institute of Certified Public Accountants. David has been published in Forbes, CNBC and other publications and is currently an active member of the Market Pulse Survey, a quarterly report of market conditions for merger and acquisition transactions.

Walter L. Lipski
Upton Financial Group
7373 E Doubletree Ranch Rd., Suite 200
Scottsdale, AZ 85258

O - 480-499-5556
D - 480-223-8060

WLipski@UptonCo.com

www.UptonCo.com
www.waltlipski.com

David G. Ryan
Upton Financial Group
131-A Stony Circle, Suite 500
Santa Rosa, CA 95401

O - 707-546-7860
D - 707-975-5540

DRyan@UptonCo.com
www.UptonCo.com

Made in the USA
Monee, IL
05 November 2026

67379324R00033